SEEDS

FOR THE

SOUL

First Sentient Publications edition 2007

A paperback original

Cover design by Timm Bryson
Book design by Adam Schnitzmeier

Library of Congress Cataloging-in-Publication Data

Hillig, Chuck.
  Seeds for the soul : living as the source of who you are / Chuck
Hillig. -- 1st Sentient Publications ed.
    p. cm.
  ISBN 978-1-59181-062-9
  1. Spiritual life. 2. Life--Religious aspects. I. Title.

BL624.H47 2007
204'.4--dc22

                                        2007038939
    Printed in the United States of America

10 9 8 7 6 5 4 3 2

SENTIENTPUBLICATIONS

A Limited Liability Company
1113 Spruce Street
Boulder, CO 80302
www.sentientpublications.com

SEEDS
FOR THE
SOUL

LIVING AS THE SOURCE
OF WHO YOU ARE

CHUCK HILLIG

SENTIENTPUBLICATIONS

All the flowers
of all the tomorrows
are in the seeds of today.

—Anonymous

Love tells me I'm everything.
Wisdom tells me I'm nothing.
Between the two, my life flows.

—Nisargadatta Maharaj

We don't see things as they are.
We see things as we are.

—Anais Nin

CONTENTS

INTRODUCTION

Frankly, I had a hard time finishing this book.

In the last few months, I had this irresistible urge to re-work the material and to fine tune either the wording or the punctuation.

Unfortunately, though, I also noticed that I was beginning to second guess myself and to create a lot of oppositional "yes, buts" to what I was saying which, of course, I then felt obliged to answer.

After a while, the whole project became more and more convoluted, and it almost seemed to be taking on a separate life of its own.

Finally, I thought, "Enough is enough! Just be done with it."

And so, one day, I just decided that it was OK that the book was perfectly imperfect.

And I just stopped writing.

Seeds for the Soul is a unique collection of ideas, speculations, thoughts, and musings, all loosely linked together by a universal worldview that is, by its very nature, quite impossible to prove.

However, since the book can be experienced on many levels, I suspect that there's something here of real value for almost everyone's taste.

You'll notice, for example, that my point of view sometimes flips back and forth between eastern philosophy and western psychology.

Who can say why? That's just what showed up.

And, along the way, I even throw in some home-grown common sense, practical advice about relationships and living in the world, semi-weird points of view about reality, some rather odd paradoxes, and even a sprinkling of curious non sequiturs.

Actually, it's really quite an interesting mixture.

So, for what it's worth, this multi-flavored banquet of soul-seeds has been laid out before you for your honest consideration, your occasional amusement, and hopefully, your heartfelt delight.

In short, I hope that it's an enriching experience.

However, a word of caution is in order here. Unlike my other three books, *Seeds for the Soul* is not meant to be a quick read.

In fact, in order to squeeze out as many of the spiritual juices that are available on these pages, I suggest that you take your time with these ideas and try to digest the seeds very slowly. Hopefully, the material itself will encourage you to occasionally pause and reflect carefully about what's being suggested or implied.

Each page has been designed to be whole and complete unto itself. Consequently, you could probably begin reading anywhere in this book, and then go exploring in either direction.

And, since this material is not being presented sequentially, some of it will deliberately double back upon itself from time to time for added clarification and review. Some things, I think, bear repeating.

One more thing. Since I'm pointing out truth on several levels of consciousness and reality, some of this material may appear to totally contradict what's already been written on other pages.

Yes, I'm very aware of the disconnects. But, as they say, one size does *not* fit all. In life, there are always layers within layers within layers.

Consequently, please don't value-judge this material too severely. As with all of my books, I'm not looking to change your beliefs about things, nor am I trying to encourage you to agree with me.

These words and ideas mean simply whatever *you* want to read into them. No more. No less.

In fact, your own personal interpretation of this material almost makes you a kind of co-creator.

Anyway, I'm not making any apology for how the book is being presented here or even for the unique format that it has finally decided to appear in.

I only know that, for some reason, these random thoughts showed up for me in my awareness over a period of several decades, and when they arrived, I felt compelled to write them down in my journals.

Who knows? Perhaps you will now feel equally compelled to make special note of some of them.

At the very least, though, I suspect that these ideas and their implications can be used as a kind of point of departure into some very fascinating discussions and debates.

But we shall see.

Anyway, it's best to consider all of these seeds as a kind of spiritual smorgasbord. However, just as you wouldn't eat something from every dish that's available on a regular buffet table, I certainly don't expect you to naively swallow absolutely everything that's being offered here.

So, before digesting any of these seeds, I encourage you instead to allow your heart to choose carefully from among these soulful delicacies.

And, finally, please don't take this book too seriously. Sometimes even *I* don't agree with absolutely everything that I write!

And so, with that sort of roundabout disclaimer, I humbly present these offerings to you from the garden of my soul.

Perhaps, if you allow these spiritual seeds to gestate for a while, the wisdom in your own soul will decide what inner fruits will be harvested from them. And when.

And so, from my garden to yours, with Love.

—Chuck Hillig

LIFE AS A GAME

*The answer
to life's problems is
to see "who" has them.*

—Ramana Maharshi

Short Definitions of Life

Much ado about nothing.

Holy shit!

Now appearing.

Nothing is written.

Nothing is seen.

Nothing doing.

The story of your life is the cosmic song of God that's being played out through the instrument of your body.

The déjà vu patterns that you're experiencing in your life play out like the repeating chorus of the song of your soul.

Even if you're able to change the words, doesn't it often seem like just another variation on the same old theme?

So here's the Big Question: Is your song happening *to* you, *for* you, *in* you, or *as* you?

You will unconsciously attract into your life those people and situations that will likely stimulate the unresolved issues of your childhood.

Life condemns you to repeat whatever it is that you didn't find the courage to fully complete.

In short, all of your past incompletions in life will always keep showing up for you.

As somebody once said, "The past isn't over. In fact, it isn't even past."

Life may not have any real meaning other than the one that you have superimposed upon it.

In short, life will tend to mean for you whatever *you* say that life means.

For example, when you say,

"Life is a drag!"
"Life is a challenge."
"Life is terrible."
"Life is a dance."
"Life is a game."
etc., etc., etc.,

then life won't disappoint you.

L ife will mysteriously show up for you in ways that fully support your heart's definition of it, no matter how self-limiting that definition might be.

But you'll have to take *some* position on it.

If you're not willing to give your life any meaning at all, then your inner fear that "My life is probably meaningless!" will automatically win by default.

Finding out about the meaning of the dramas in your life has a whole lot to do with discovering what you've been unconsciously priming yourself to receive.

Perhaps an even deeper purpose of life, though, is to eventually discover that you're only pretending that life even *has* some kind of deeper purpose or meaning that you can eventually discover.

Maybe the initial discovery is in seeing that you've only been on a treadmill to nowhere.

Maybe, in the end, life is just the way that it is.

Guidelines for Life

Show up.
Pay attention.
Tell the truth.
Don't judge.
Be compassionate.

Express silent gratitude to everyone for showing up in your dream. (After all, they're only here to support your own awakening.)

Above all, don't be attached to the *results* of your efforts.

There are only two real choices:

1. Resist what shows up for you in life and then, grudgingly, finally learn to accept it, or

2. Consciously *choose* what shows up for you in life and then, lovingly, embrace it being just as it is.

The problems in your life are in direct proportion to your unwillingness to swallow absolutely *everything* that's on your path.

The problem is *not* in what's showing up for you.

The problem is in your *resistance* to what's showing up for you.

It's in your shouting out to the cosmos, "This should *not* be so!"

When you swallow the entire you-niverse, then you're not resisting what is.

If you're patient, though, then *everything* that shows up for you will eventually become edible.

However, don't expect it all to taste just like dessert!

You're unconsciously attracting in life whatever it is that you've been trying to avoid or deny.

But no matter what shows up for you, it's only there for your growth and edification.

However, just because everything in life is a *gift*, it doesn't mean that it's going to be a *toy*.

Either *use* life, or life will end up using—or even abusing—you for *not* using it.

Resign yourself graciously to how life really is.

Surrendering is very different than submitting, just like how giving *up* is very different than giving *in*.

One is involuntary while the other one is voluntary.

But, you'll *still* have to take your lumps.

Sooner or later, life humiliates us all.

You're living out your life by unconsciously reacting to what you've purposefully forgotten that you already *are*.

Throughout your entire life, you will probably remember, and then forget, this same truth, again and again and again.

Just as the depth of your sleep cycle varies throughout the night, so will you also feel clearer and more spiritually awake at certain times in your life than you will at other times.

Allow yourself to comfortably move in and out of your uncomfortable confusion.

And remember, "This, too, shall pass."

To live your life intensely and on the edge-of-the-wedge, act as if you're experiencing everything that shows up for you for the very last time.

Obviously, sooner or later, this will certainly be true.

Then every conversation, every cup of tea, every bird in flight, etc., becomes a cause and an opportunity for celebration and gratitude.

Create deep passion in your life for something heartfelt, and then stay fully committed to it.

Taking a stand in life is even more important than the nature of the particular stand that you're taking.

Amazingly, the universe doesn't really care *what* you want to get committed to.

It just doesn't like you to be wishy-washy.

B e more willing to fully live the risk that life is.

But remember: there are *no* guarantees.

In short, you could be doing everything "right" and *still* get hurt.

No matter what happens in life, it's still OK, even if it doesn't always feel that way to you.

But, since there are no mistakes in life, then even thinking that there *are* mistakes in life isn't really a mistake, is it?

The Mystery of Life: The indivisible *pretends* to be divisible, assumes a point of view, and then struggles to seemingly regain what it had never really lost.

You're not moving through life like walking through some kind of elaborate maze.

You're actually standing perfectly still, and life's maze is really moving through *you*.

So, be a-mazed!

Your life is an incredible gift that you're giving to yourself, so don't squander it.

Dance the dance!

As someone once said, "The living are few; the dead are many."

Your life's journey is a pilgrimage that's always going from one sacred space to yet another sacred space.

And the very road that you're traveling on between these sacred spaces is *also* sacred.

No matter *what* your life looks like right now, you're always standing in the Temple of the Divine.

Your own Heart is truly the Holy-of-Holies.

Your life's story becomes melodramatic when it's mostly about how *you* are "right" and about how others have "wronged" you.

But, in truth, the painful events in your life have not been happening *to* you.

They've only been happening *for* you.

Nobody judges an artist's painting before it's complete.

Likewise, since your life is also a kind of work of art in progress, don't judge it before it's finished.

You can have more fun in the great play of life by becoming a wonderfully memorable character in everyone *else's* melodrama.

Learn to roll with your role.

WHO IS RESPONSIBLE?

*Do your duty
and leave the rest to Heaven.*

—Corneille

As long as you believe that you're a separate ego, the universe will hold you personally responsible for absolutely everything that you think, feel, say, and do.

In life, there are neither victors *nor* victims.

If you're an adult and are still feeling emotionally victimized by others, then you're in an unconscious co-conspiracy with them to be victimized.

In short, others will tend to sell what *you* will tend to buy.

O f all of the people that you'll ever meet in your life, *you* are the only one that you will never leave—or lose.

To the questions in your life, *you* are the only answer.

To the problems in your life, *you* are the only solution.

You're ultimately responsible for making all of your own choices, even if you choose to not be responsible for making *any* of them.

This means that you're also 100 percent responsible for the maintenance of your own sense of self worth.

If you get strokes from anyone else, then that's just the frosting on the cake.

You are still responsible for baking the cake of self-esteem yourself.

You're always doing *exactly* what you want to be doing, 100 percent of the time.

There aren't any exceptions.

And, since you're always able to choose your own responses, you are considered response-able.

In other words—*responsible*.

If you're not having a good time in your life, then perhaps you've forgotten *how* you've created your current situation and just why you've brought it onto your path.

In life, there are only two things that you absolutely *have* to do:

1. Make decisions. (You cannot *not* decide.)

2. Die. (Nobody ever gets out alive.)

Everything else, however, is optional.

B ut let's say that someone kidnaps you, and then drops you off in the middle of the desert.

Although you're not responsible for getting yourself taken *to* the desert, you're still 100 percent responsible for getting yourself *out* of the desert.

Just because someone abused you as a kid, you're still responsible for your *own* healing.

And, yes, I know you might think that it's unfair.

However, life doesn't really care what you *think*. Life only cares what you *believe*.

And it certainly doesn't care if you like how it is, if you understand how it is or even if you agree with how it is.

Life's going to do exactly what it wants to do, whether *you* are aboard or not.

So, since you can't get with what isn't, you'd better start learning to get with what *is*.

Don't rescue anyone by trying to do their inner work for them.

You'll only be discounting their strength and discouraging them from developing their own untapped resources.

Instead, give yourself permission to allow them to completely and totally fail—if failing seems to be what's on their path.

If you keep handing someone a crutch, they'll surely learn how to limp.

WHAT DO YOU BELIEVE?

Actions themselves form no bondage.
Bondage is only the false belief
"I am the do-er."

—Ramana Maharshi

H owever you believe the world to be, that's *exactly* how the world will present itself to you.

You are always living your life out *into* your beliefs about how life is.

You'll see something in your life whenever you begin to *believe* it strongly enough.

It's not the other way around.

In fact, you're creating your own private hell every day through your attachment to your belief that *this*, right here and right now, is *not* heaven.

Your strongest held beliefs about how things are will draw into your life those very experiences that will work to support and prove your strongest held beliefs about how things are.

The universe loves you so completely that it's *compelled* to present itself to you in ways that will tend to validate your strongest held beliefs, no matter how self-limiting or off-the-wall those beliefs might be.

In short, the universe wants to make you *right*.

I f you want to create new results in your life, then you'll have to change your old beliefs.

You can't get to the new results that you *want* from the old beliefs that you *have.*

Unfortunately, many of your beliefs about yourself depend on what you believe others may be believing about you.

Someone else's opinion of you should only be looked at as interesting information to be considered.

Nothing more.

The final judgment about yourself is only for *you* to make.

FEAR OF DESIRE—
DESIRE FOR FEAR

*Securities, certitudes and peace
do not lead to discoveries.*

—Carl Jung

The cosmic dance that's generated between what you *fear* and what you *desire* provides both the energy and the momentum to keep your game in (e)motion.

Fear (yin) and desire (yang), however, are but different sides of the same cosmic coin.

Although they've each taken root in the very heart of their opposite, they still appear to chase each other around the famous symbol of yin-yang.

In truth, though, they're really the very best of friends.

Your belief that something is missing in the present moment provides the momentum for the melodrama of your life to propel itself outward in search of this absent and elusive *something*.

Similarly, the proverbial donkey is never able to arrive at the dangling carrot because the carrot is always kept just out of its reach.

Just like it is for you.

Life's ongoing momentum prevents you from reaching any *permanent* satisfaction or experiencing any sense of final completion.

Sadly, though, you never seem to run out of new carrots to dangle in front of your ravishing "I's."

t's in your nature to create, and you'll always create *exactly* what you desire.

Amazingly, this is *still* true even when what's showing up for you is a lot of fear.

Fear returns to your life more often whenever you forget how you, yourself, keep inviting it to join you again.

When fear shows up, though, it's sometimes helpful to invite it to come very close. Let it whisper softly in your ear and tell you what it *truly* wants.

You may not always like what it says to you.

But, if your heart is open to hearing the awful truth, fear will bring you gifts of self-discovery.

Just beyond the fear awaits the treasure.

What do you want that you're not getting?

What are you getting that you don't want?

It's best to always focus your energies on what you deeply desire.

So, unless you secretly want it, stop focusing on what you *don't* want.

If you're not actively moving towards what you *desire*, then you'll likely be sliding backwards into what you *fear*.

Both your fear and your desire have their roots in your belief that something needs to be added *to*, or subtracted *from*, the present moment in order to make it, somehow, "better."

Actually, things won't ever get any better.

They'll just get more, *or less*, comfortable.

In the end, though, things are just as they are.

ince they're both focused on the future, fear and desire arise simultaneously in your heart.

Contained within every desire, however, is a hidden *fear* that it won't happen.

Paradoxically, though, contained within every fear is also a hidden *desire* that it won't happen.

Your fears will begin to diminish whenever you stop feeding your desires.

And, of course, vice versa.

Fears and desires always eat from the same trough.

O ur psychological work has to do with fear while our spiritual work has to do with love.

Fear excludes and says,

No!

Love, however, includes and says,

Yes!

Your fear is always built around your resistance to letting go.

Because fear contracts around itself, it works to shrink the size of your world.

Love, however, works to expand it.

Whatever you're fearfully resisting in life is also fearfully resisting *you*.

Whatever you're saying no to in life, is also saying no to you.

Consequently, when you're not fighting *yourself* as *you* truly are, then you're much less likely to be fighting others as *they* truly are.

When you're willing to say an unqualified yes to whatever is showing up for you, then everything that shows up is *always* OK.

But, even if you say no to something, you'll still be OK if you're willing to say yes to the fact that, at least for right now, you're saying no.

As long as the very *last* word that you say to the universe is,

Yes!

Paradoxically, your fears will begin to diminish in intensity as soon as you're willing to create space in your life for yourself to occasionally become very fearful.

The problem is *not* being afraid.

The problem is being afraid of being afraid.

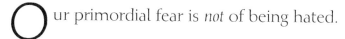

Our primordial fear is *not* of being hated.

In fact, it's just the opposite.

Our primordial fear is actually of being loved so *completely* that our experience of separation from others will dissolve entirely and we'll disappear.

The ego's survival depends on the existence of the other. In fact, that's exactly what makes the other so very significant.

We just don't want to be alone.

Ironically, our outer fear of being alone is only an external manifestation of the *inner* fear of being all-one.

A nything that you stand in opposition to, you'll be afraid of.

In other words, if there is no "not-I," then there is no fear.

However, fear serves a very important purpose.

Your fearful opposition to the not-I actually protects you from the danger of being personally annihilated by the pure light of unconditional love.

Creating conflict in the world serves to distract you from the terrifying fear of disappearing into the profound stillness of who you really are.

In the long run, though, the busy-ness that the mind creates concerning the other still won't be able to prevent the final ego dissolution from eventually taking place.

W hat usually stops you from waking up is your deep-rooted fear of death.

However, a fear of dying often disguises an un-conscious fear of really *living*.

The soul's release lies in discovering that this illu-sory "you" has never really lived in the first place, and so, consequently, it can never really die.

Fearing death is really like fearing to wake up from a dream.

But after you awaken, your dream characters are then looked upon very differently.

In both cases, though, you're only dreaming about your own disguised (or disowned) self.

The more that you see yourself as being *away* from the heart of who you really are, the greater will be your fear.

But, how can "who you are" ever really move away from itself at all?

The center of the universe lies in the very heart of your own heart.

I n spite of your beliefs to the contrary, you are *not* what you think, feel, say, do, have, want, or fear.

You're actually the *context* or the space in which all of those other things appear to show up.

In short, you are "what is."

You are what creates you.

It's all happening both within, and *as, you.*

So, instead of *reacting* out of your fear, you need to learn how to *respond* out of your love.

Romantics are always looking for The One.

But, everywhere you go, you're always (and *only*) meeting The One.

Every one is The One.

We create fear by telling ourselves scary stories about what *might* happen in the future.

If your daily focus is mostly on what *may* be coming down the road for you, then fear will be your constant companion.

Stay present in the present.

Practice being non-judgmental.

It'll be much easier for all of us to be *with* each other as soon as we become more willing to stop being *at* each other.

Anyway, we're much more alike than not.

Don't we all laugh, cry, sneeze, scream, burp, smile, cough, and fart in the same language?

As long as you blame your past tragedies for your current life's condition, you will continue to avoid feeling your fear of acknowledging your personal responsibility for *changing* those conditions.

Blaming others traps *everyone*.

Holding others responsible for their behaviors, however, releases people to act responsibly.

The story of your past abuse is just one of many books in the vast library that you are.

Start reading (and writing) newer books with happier storylines.

Don't make your past wounding be the central theme of your whole life.

Right now, you're only here to give love, to forgive fear, and to dance!

If God forgives everyone, who are you *not* to?

Forgiving yourself (and others) for how you *were* will make it much easier for you to forgive yourself (and others) for how you *are*.

Your burning desire to be perfect often disguises your fear of it being discovered that you might, somehow, be imperfect.

But everything is *always* perfectly perfect being just exactly as it is.

In fact, things can't be other than how they are right now because, for whatever reason, the conditions for them to be different just didn't show up.

Perfection is *always* present for you the very moment that you give up your idea about what perfection should look like.

Perfection looks exactly like *this*.

As long as you're dreaming that you're awake, there'll be no end to your fears or your desires.

They will only end when you become fully awakened to your own dreaming.

Suffering finds its roots in your desire to be free from something that's present, even if it's only a desire to be free from dreaming the Dream.

But no desire is really spiritual, including the so-called spiritual desire to have *no* spiritual desires.

And yet, paradoxically, it's *all* absolutely spiritual.

Yes! *All of it.*

Every fear. Every desire.

Internal conflict arises in your heart whenever desire and fear refer to the same object.

It's the desire to eat vs. the fear of it all being gone.

Painful experiences in your melodrama are often triggered by your desire to cling to something that's going away and your unspoken fear that it might not ever come again.

As you step further away from the tapestry of your life, though, you'll see how desire and fear have become deeply interwoven into your fabric again and again.

Crisscrossing many times, over and over, their weaving works to form the very patterns of your life.

D esires are only diversions that seduce us until we finally recognize their illusory core.

You have to give up *all* hope that "wonderful things will soon be happening for me."

Hope focuses on a future where you believe that things will somehow get much better for you.

Such a desire, though, subtly discounts the present moment of Now by seeing it only as a stepping stone to another time in the distant future where you may, *finally*, become happy.

But, ironically, if you're not fully satisfied in this present moment, then you'll *never* be fully satisfied *anywhere*.

There's no final resolution in life because everything in life is *already* being fully resolved, moment to moment.

Look around you. Right now, *this* is how life is fully resolving itself.

Amazingly, there are no *other* moments waiting in the future for you to be living into.

This very moment, *right now*, is really *it*.

Unless you develop true intimacy with what's *real*, then you'll always be struggling with both your fears and your desires.

But your heart can't be *truly* intimate with either fear or desire.

Your heart can only be truly intimate with *who you really are*.

U nconditional love is the opposite of both fear and desire.

Unlike them, though, unconditional love has absolutely nothing to lose and nothing to gain.

Consequently, it's not moving either towards something or away from something.

Although it may make common distinctions in the world of forms, unconditional love is unwilling to make any judgmental conclusions about any of them.

Because of this, unconditional love always says no to nothing and yes to *everything*.

The *I am* is that which makes all life possible.

The *I am* cleverly uses fear and desire to pretend that the there and then—what *isn't*—is somehow better than the here and now—what *is*.

However, if spiritual enlightenment is the sum of all desires, then by contrast, the *final* (and inevitable) annihilation of the personal ego is truly the sum of all fears.

LOVE,
RELATIONSHIPS,
AND THERAPY

Love is the pursuit of the whole.

—Plato

The heart of good therapy lies in creating a safe space for yourself to fully *complete* your relationships with life, with others, and with yourself.

Your healing depends on finding the courage to face and embrace the unvarnished truth—including *all* of the warts—about life, about others and, especially, about *yourself.*

There are no easy Cliff Notes for knowing how to live life.

There are only cliffs.

Some you have to walk along.

Some you have to walk around.

Some you have to climb.

Some you have to fall off of.

T herapy is the gentle art of leading you back to a fuller and richer experience of yourself.

Unconditional love, on the other hand, leads you back to a fuller and richer experience of your own true *nature*.

Therapy focuses on seeking completion within the *world* while spirituality focuses on discovering completion within your *Heart*.

Breakdowns in both areas, however, often precede break-*throughs*.

D o you have the courage to ask 100 percent of the people for 100 percent of what you want 100 percent of the time?

If not, then you'll be requiring others to magically read your mind.

In speaking your own truth, you sometimes need to be willing to say no to what other people want.

However, you'll be less willing to *say* no to others unless you're also willing to *hear* no from others, too.

Give yourself permission to check everything out first before assuming *anything* about anyone else.

If you don't find that courage, then your private theories about what's going on for other people will secretly run, and occasionally *ruin*, your relationships with them.

Good advice: *Always check it out.*

The cup of your most significant relationships will be both a golden chalice and an iron cauldron.

P ut most of your attention on what's *working* between the two of you and not on what's *not* working.

In short, make sure that you're watering the *flowers* in the relationship and not, indirectly, watering the *weeds*.

Above all, recognize that you don't always need to solve or heal *everything* the exact moment that it shows up for you.

Instead, allow it to get a bit uncomfortable.

Sometimes all that's required to nourish your relationship with another is your heart's willingness to be fully present for them as a silent witness to the telling of their truth.

J ust because you *feel* like doing something evil, it doesn't mean that you absolutely *have* to do it.

Deeply hidden within our souls, we *all* have these secret pockets of pathology.

All of them, however, must be fully acknowledged, respected, honored, and embraced.

Notice your own craziness, and then move on.

Most of our problems with other human beings usually start with our *own* problems with just being human.

In relationships, you're always attracting what-ever it is that you've disowned in yourself.

You will, for example, unconsciously re-create situations that remind you of your past unre-solved issues concerning engulfment and aban-donment.

When you contaminate your relationships with your own issues, it's sometimes helpful to give them the space to *not* work very well from time to time.

If you don't consciously provide that space, then your relationships will often seem to *not* work a *lot* more often.

Your relationships must first be experienced the way that they currently *are* before space can be created for them to be experienced the way that they currently *aren't*.

After all, first things first.

You'll *like* those others who will help your ego to constantly reinforce its separation from the world.

However, you'll deeply *love* those others whose way of being occasionally triggers a surrendering of your own ego—no matter how momentary that surrendering might be.

This is also why we deeply love our great masterpieces of art. For a brief, cathartic moment, their power can short-circuit the ego and dissolve our illusion of separation.

Since the effect is indescribable, we then end up worshiping the vehicle that seemingly has just opened our heart, be it human or human-made.

In one-on-one relationships, however, you'll also need to have trust, intimacy, and commitment.

Love, by itself, just isn't a good enough reason to stay together.

After all, you don't live with everyone you love.

Your capacity to love others and yourself is directly proportional to your willingness to forgive others and yourself.

For example, instead of loving the parents that you *wanted*, start learning to love the parents that you *have*.

To heal from past trauma, you'll need to first get angry, grieve the losses and finally, forgive them all.

You can't completely forgive anyone until you're willing to voluntarily walk away from your right for revenge and retribution forever.

You don't forgive others in order to heal *them*.

You forgive others in order to heal *yourself*.

A lthough we have an absolute need to love others, we don't really get to choose *how* love wants to express itself through us.

Because it deprives our own Heart from spiritual nourishment, deliberately withholding our love from another is really the gravest of sins.

Love itself is so much greater than any of the relationships that it shows up in.

In the end, the greatest lesson will be in learning to love your partner *more* than you love the *form* of the relationship that you're having with them.

True compassion allows space for others to fulfill their own destiny without imposing on their process *any* demands, no matter how reasonable those demands might be, as to how they should be unfolding.

Don't judge others.

We're always doing the very best that we're capable of at any given moment in space and time.

Criticizing another person is a lot like seeing your *own* dirty face reflected in the mirror, and then washing the mirror!

D on't ever think that you're any better than anyone else.

After all, an author loves his nasty villains every bit as much as he loves his courageous heroes.

Honor the cosmic play by becoming an appreciative (and very grateful) audience to your own melodrama.

Paradoxically, you can be 100 percent engaged in your drama while still being 100 percent *detached* from it.

Just because the hole may be *in* the paper, it doesn't also mean that the hole is really *of* the paper.

In it, but not *of* it.

You'll automatically find along your path whatever props that you'll need in order to play out your scenes on the stage of your life.

If something (like wealth, fame, power, etc.) has not shown up for you in life in spite of your best efforts, then trust that you won't need it in order to successfully play out your role.

In fact, your heart will unconsciously sabotage your ego's attempts to get any of those things.

Seven words to live by:

Serve others.

Trust your self.

Love God.

The problem is not that you don't know *how* to love yourself.

The problem is in acknowledging that, deep down, you may not be completely *willing* to do so.

However, when you're willing to unconditionally love someone, the total absence of your ego attachment can lead you to experiencing true Presence in your relationship.

And it's a Presence that doesn't also have the added burden of carrying and defending a personal identity.

At the bottom line, it's all just Love—loving *Itself*. Love is not a place where you're going to.

L ove is actually the very place where you're coming from.

Love is really *who* you really are.

Absolutely everything that occurs in life is a perfect expression of the unconditional love that Consciousness has for Itself.

Unfortunately, the judgmental ego often says "Love shouldn't look like this! Love should look more like that!"

Actually, love should, and does, look *exactly* like what's happening.

It's *all* only love, even if *you* don't recognize it as such.

In fact, love is even big enough to contain your own non-recognition of it.

B ecause it desperately needs to perceive separation, the ego has a very limited capacity to
love.

For this very same reason, however, it also has a
very great capacity to be *afraid*.

If the ego is involved, then the love around it is
always *conditional*.

We can't unconditionally love anyone that we either need or resist.

We should sing *with* them, not cling *to* them.

Only the unconditional love of a Beloved can help
you to transcend both fear and desire.

The Beloved is often the final portal leading to the
dissolution of the ego.

And, in the end, the Beloved then disappears into
Itself.

When love recycles itself *as* love, then the universe appears.

In truth, the visible world is only a physical manifestation of love loving itself.

Everyone in your life has shown up for you in order to play in your play.

And you're always swimming in their love, even if it doesn't always seem that way to you.

Since God equals Love, then saying "I love you" actually means "I *god* you."

God it?

Or, if you "loved" here, you'd be Om by now.

But, don't worry.

Sooner or later, we're all going Om.

SO WHAT'S REALLY TRUE?

The truth shall make you free.

—John 8:32

By telling the truth about who you are, moment to moment, you're also creating a safe space for others to tell you their truth about who *they* are, moment to moment.

But *you* need to find the courage to go *first*.

If you don't tell your truth to others, then you're left with only being able to tell your *lie*.

Take your pick.

E very conscious denial of your truth auto-matically triggers a compensatory response in your own soul.

When you lie to yourself about what's so for you, then that part of you that knows the *real* truth tends to go unconscious and to split off from your own awareness.

However, that disowned part of you is then com-pelled to struggle for greater recognition by open-ly asserting the *real* truth, and sometimes in very uncomfortable ways.

Whatever is being denied only wants to bring its unacknowledged presence into *full* conscious-ness for you to experience, and then to eventu-ally claim.

Sooner or later, the unknown shall be made known.

Sooner or later, the hidden gets tired of hiding.

E very single moment, you have the choice to either lie about what's so for you or to tell the absolute truth about it and risk the consequences that come with just being who, and how, you are.

Either express your truth with integrity, or you'll depress your heart with certainty.

If your outsides don't match your insides, then you're not being fully authentic in the world.

You're just trying to look good.

When you lie about your inner truth, you're not only disempowering yourself, you're also subtly discounting the strength of the listener.

You're implying that they're just not strong enough, or smart enough (or *whatever* enough) to be able to handle the hearing of your truth.

But when I hold *you* responsible for my own unwillingness to share my truth, then I'm also likely to blame you for my own fear, too.

Consequently, if I don't find the courage to speak the truth, my emotional blockages will create a kind of psychic constipation in my gut.

For the soul, truth-telling is the best laxative.

You will never know the Truth.

You can only *be* the Truth.

There is no knower that's really separate from the Truth that's being known.

The ego says that it wants to experience the Truth, but it survives more by saying no to the truth than it does by saying yes to it.

However, Consciousness *is* truth itself, and so it needs no one present in order to validate it.

Life is just as it is.

There's nothing *more* than just this.

And, quite amazingly, there's nothing *else* than just this.

W hat you really want is to have a profound experience of your own true nature.

At the deepest level, you are compelled to seek out the true Source of who you really are.

The irony, though, is that when you seemingly arrive at the very core of your Being, there'll be *nobody* there to greet you.

Who you *think* you are can't possibly survive your own awakening.

Nobody can survive it.

The Great Paradox: There's nothing that's *you* and, at the very same time, there's nothing that's *not* you.

Here's the height of spiritual irony: The teacher points directly to the Truth, but then the student begins worshipping the *teacher*.

Or, even worse, the student begins to worship the *pointer* that the teacher was using!

But, as Consciousness Itself *you* are really the ultimate Source of *all* of the great teachers.

You are really the ultimate Source of *all* of their spiritual teachings.

You only created them in your personal drama to remind you, again and again, about what you're pretending to forget.

The teachers and their teachings both appear (and disappear) within the heart of who *you* are.

A common mistake is in believing that *you* are the original Singer-of-the-Song of your life.

Even though you're really only lip-synching the words, you're still trying to take the credit (or the blame) for the song that's being sung.

And, ironically, you're still responsible for all of your choices, even though you don't seem to have any control over making them.

Responsibility, but no blame.

However, there will still be consequences.

A lthough the Truth shall be known in the twinkling of an "I," you do not hold the Truth.

In fact, it's just the opposite.

The Truth is really holding *you*.

And the Truth is absolutely perfect right here and right now.

And it's always perfecting itself, *perfectly*.

There are *never* any mistakes.

Not ever!

Everyone already knows their part in the great Dance of Life.

Who does what and to whom has *already*, and *always*, been decided.

In short, justice is whatever happens.

Your resistance to your truth will invite into your life whatever it is that you've been avoiding.

In fact, your denial of what's really true for you will delay what *isn't* true (the changes that you want to make in your life) from ever showing up.

If you deny your truth, then you're stuck with only being able to defend your lie.

But, in the end, you can't run from yourself, and you can't hide.

You already *are* who it is that you'd be hiding from, and you're also where it is that you'd be running to.

You can't escape your Self any more than you can escape your own Shadow.

Try as it might, the wave can never leave the ocean.

The world doesn't owe you a living.

After all, wasn't the world already going on when you, mysteriously, showed up in it?

Actually, though, "who you are" was going on *long* before the world showed up—in *you*.

Yes, who you are really came *first*.

And the world *still* doesn't owe you a living!

When you resist what's true for you when it's gently knocking on the door of your heart, then it will soon begin to *pound*.

If you're still unwilling to acknowledge its presence, those denied energies will begin to set up a siege around your life.

No matter how horrible it is, your disowned truth only wants to be looked at, acknowledged, honored, respected, and embraced.

It absolutely *hates* to be ignored!

Give it what it wants (see above), and then let it go out the back door!

You already *are* the very Beloved that you've been seeking.

Although there seems to be separate personalities in the world, there's really no separate person.

There's only One.

But it's a One without a *some*-one being attached to it.

Because of this, no matter where it is that you rest your gaze, you're always looking directly into the multi-faceted Face of God.

And, miraculously, it's always been your very *own* face.

Give up your idea about what you and God seem to look like.

You both look *exactly* like what is.

FEELINGS? YES!

Sour, sweet, bitter, pungent:
all must be tasted.

—A Chinese proverb

Your feelings don't really hassle you.

What hassles you are your *beliefs* about what you think you *should* be feeling instead of what you actually *are* feeling.

In other words, you're should-ing all over yourself!

Your hassles only increase when you feel angry about your anger, sad about your sadness, fearful about your fear, distressed about your distress, guilty about your guilt, ashamed about your shame, etc., etc., etc.

Give yourself 100 percent permission to feel *whatever* is showing up for you.

You don't have to feel lousy about feeling lousy.

Just feel lousy.

Your uncomfortable feelings will change *faster* as soon as you stop trying so hard to change them.

You don't need to understand your feelings before you give yourself the OK to fully experience them.

In fact, you're likely to remain *stuck* in a painful feeling whenever you don't give yourself complete permission to have being-stuck-in-a-painful-feeling as your truth for that moment.

Since figuring out your feelings is *not* a prerequisite, no explanations for their appearance on your path are ever required.

They're there simply because they're there.

Period.

Your feelings are not problems to be solved, obstacles to be overcome or difficulties to be denied.

They're only passing phenomena on your path that are inviting you to experience them fully.

But don't turn down their invitation. If you won't let them be as they are, they won't let *you* be as *you* are.

For example, if you ignore your feelings when they show up for you on the doorstep of your heart, they'll surely hassle you for your lack of respect.

They'll disappear into your unconscious for a while, but when they come back to you (and they will) they'll be bringing some friends!

Your thoughts and feelings are a lot like the 88 notes on a piano.

You can make sounds by striking the keys on the keyboard.

However, you can only make real *music* by first getting on, and then off, these very same keys, second by second, over and over.

Likewise, in order to fully play out the song that you are, you need to first acknowledge and experience *each* of your thoughts and feelings.

But then, of course, you need to be willing to give them all up and to move on to what's *next*.

Get *on* them.

And then get *off* them.

Over and over.

I f you don't own *all* of your own feelings, they'll end up owning you!

If you're not willing to let go of your feelings after they arise in you, then they won't be very willing to let go of *you*.

Instead, you'll end up re-playing the same emotional notes in your life again, and again, and again, and again.

Focus your attention on the music that the Cosmos has placed in front of *you* and become more willing to fully participate in the cosmic orchestra.

Play *all* of your *own* notes, and don't leave anything out.

Then turn the page and move on!

There's a big difference between you as the musician and the music that you're playing in the cosmic orchestra.

Sometimes, you'll all play together.

Sometimes, though, you'll be required to play all alone.

And sometimes you'll just be expected to sit there quietly and do absolutely *nothing*.

But even your silence is part of your music.

T here are no good feelings, and there are no bad feelings.

Feelings should only be classified as being comfortable or uncomfortable.

Labeling feelings as bad will only lessen your willingness to associate yourself with them when they show up for you.

Judging your feelings as bad is an indirect way of judging *yourself* as bad for having them being present in your life.

Resisting life, however, only stokes the fire.

The Universe just doesn't like to hear "no."

If you're not willing to really feel your emotional pain, then you're not going to be feeling much of anything else, either.

When you're deeply sad, become willing to cry tearfully on your cheeks.

Even if you try keeping your pain hidden inside, sooner or later, you'll still have to cry it all out.

Only this time, your tears will be on your *soul*.

You are the true source of all of your own experiences in life.

Since it's all *your* drama, you're even the true source of whatever it is that you're feeling victimized by.

In other words, no one else is *making* you think or feel anything. They're just *inviting* you to create some experience for yourself, and then *you* are taking them up on their offer.

You can change your feelings by learning how to change your *focus*.

Your experiences in life are ultimately determined by *where* you're putting your full awareness.

In the end, your heart will *always* walk towards whatever it is that your mind is paying attention to.

The purpose of therapy is *not* to get you to feel better.

The purpose of therapy is to provide a safe space for you to tell the truth, feel what you're feeling, embrace the nature of who and how you are and to come to terms with accepting the sometimes harsh realities of life itself.

The goal in therapy is *not* to help you to be free *of* uncomfortable feelings.

The goal is to help you to be free *from* uncomfortable feelings.

Not emotion-*less*, but emotion-*free*.

SEEDS FOR THE SOUL

The psychologist says, "*Own* your own feelings."

The Guru says, "*Be* the very space in which your feelings are arising."

Consciousness says, "Exactly *who* is the one who is doing all of this feeling, anyway?"

The Original Thinker (Consciousness) is only thinking *one* thought:

"I am."

All other thoughts are only secondary variations of this one Prime Thought.

The Original Feeler (also Consciousness) is only feeling *one* feeling:

Unconditional love.

All other feelings are only secondary variations of this one Prime Feeling.

J ust because you think (or feel) that something is true, it still doesn't make it true.

Thoughts and feelings exist *only* in the "I" of the Beholder.

They have no other reality.

They act like decorative ornaments that randomly hang on the tree of your ego.

Without their razzle-dazzle, the tree would not be able to be seen.

Without the tree, however, these ornaments would really have nothing to hang from.

The *appearance* of the ego is *not* being denied.

What *is* being denied, however, is its reality.

Likewise, the thoughts and feelings that show up for you are very real.

What's *not* real, however, is a separate "you" who is actually the ultimate, creative Source of these thoughts and feelings.

Here's the Great Mystery:

Yes, there are thoughts—but there's no thinker.

Yes, there are feelings—but there's no feeler.

Yes, there are words—but there's no speaker.

Yes, there are actions—but there's no do-er.

TAKING ACTION IN
THE WORLD

Things are not worth attending to;
yet they have to be attended to.

—Lao Tzu

Although you don't have any real control, it still appears to be very important that you *pretend* that you do.

Some people say, "I'll begin to act as soon as I begin to feel better."

Actually, you'll probably begin to feel better as soon as you begin to *act*.

So, take action *first*, or, at least, *pretend* that you're taking action.

Then, if it's appropriate, make your mid-course corrections along the way.

And, of course, always trust in the Process.

The "path" to your own awakening is best honored through your active participation in, and with, the very illusions that you've created around you.

So, if you're feeling compelled to protect the environment, save the whales, feed the hungry, etc., then go ahead and really throw yourself into it.

Don't hold *anything* back. Do it 100 percent!

However, just don't get attached to demanding that certain *results* show up because of your efforts.

Inner peace is possible *only* in your willingness to become completely comfortable with *every* possible outcome.

Yes, even the most painful ones.

You can't go to heaven unless you're *also* willing to go to hell.

However, trying to radically change a difficult situation sometimes only makes it much worse.

Maybe all that's required to transform what's going on in the present moment is your willingness just to be *with* it for a while.

Being with it, though, means that you're always willing to say yes to everything first.

Saying yes to what is recognizes that *all* change can only take place from where you're currently *at*.

In other words, by saying yes to something first, you're then creating the possibility of, perhaps, saying no later on.

After all, why would you bother saying no to something that you weren't willing to acknowledge was even present for you?

Saying yes *always* comes before saying no.

C an you become so much at peace that if you stopped right now and took no further action whatsoever, your entire life would still be perfectly whole and complete?

In other words, can you get to a place in your heart where there's no more *forward momentum?*

A place that you don't need to move away from in order to feel satisfied or improved?

A peaceful place where each and every moment, no matter *what* is happening, is a separate and unique destination in and of itself and, as such, is completely worthy of joyous celebration?

True peace has no inner momentum.

True peace is not going anywhere.

True peace forms the context in which *both* happiness and unhappiness show up.

True peace is *always* at peace, even when it's un-happy.

In fact, it's at peace even when it's at war.

When "what isn't" is chosen over "what is," then things appear to move.

Movement, however, doesn't necessarily mean that things are changing, and it certainly doesn't mean that anything is being improved.

The Great Mystery is discovered only in seeing the inaction *within* the action, and, at the same time, seeing the action *within* the inaction.

Action vs. Inaction

The Psychologist says "Do."

The Guru says "Be."

Consciousness, taking both positions, says "Do-Be-Do-Be-Do."

But, once again, all change is Go(o)d.

Sooner or later, the cosmic kaleidoscope is always re-cycling everything and creating *new* mandalas.

Same stones.

Different patterns.

Actually, "you" aren't really going anyplace, and "you" aren't really doing anything.

There's no *other* place for you to go to, and there's nothing else for you to be doing.

In fact, there's really nobody who's *ever* going anywhere, and there's really nobody who's *ever* doing anything. No body at all.

It's your nature to think that there's a world out there, and that there's a separate person called you that's walking through it.

However, *you* are not the thinker. Consciousness thinks, and you, as the ego, *seem* to be having the thoughts. But, relax. Since it's all only One, you can't move closer to God with your sanctity nor further away with your depravity. In Consciousness, there's just no coming or going.

Compassion and love slowly awaken the dreamer, while anger and fear only tend to deepen the dreaming.

You have your beliefs just like you have your clothes.

However, you are *not* your beliefs just like you're not your clothes.

Both your clothes and your beliefs can always be changed.

Taking a rigid stand on any of your beliefs, though, only triggers yet another question: "Well, then, what is my stand standing on?"

And on and on. Ad infinitum.

Asking such unanswerable questions only fuels the hope of finding a satisfactory answer at sometime in the future.

The quality of the questions you ask shapes the quality of the answers that are eventually provided.

"Who am I?" and "How can I make more money?" are really the same question at very different levels.

Until your Soul finally runs out of *all* of its questions, though, you'll always be on the Search.

SURRENDER? ME?!

Each one's destiny cannot be altered.

—Chuang Tzu

B efore you cross the threshold into dreamless sleep, absolutely *everything* in the world that you hold near and dear will have to be surrendered and left behind.

You can only enter that empty kingdom with empty hands, empty mind, and an empty heart.

If you're coming with anything in your hands, mind, or heart, you're required to wait at the threshold until you finally put it down.

Even in the waking world, surrendering fully to how life really *is* also requires that, sometimes, you sit quietly in the middle of your mess and in the core of your chaos, and just wait.

Wait—with *no* expectations.

Wait—in your own emptiness.

D ivine power has to be completely non-directed.

In the act of surrender, there can never be a forcing.

Trying to *will* a release only makes the release become tighter.

Releasing does not yield to will.

Releasing only yields to *yielding*.

Fulfill your role in the Great Play, no matter *what* that is, with complete gratitude and total joy.

Play your role out to its fullest.

In fact, if you *fully* surrender to what is, you don't even have to pray.

But *awakening* won't offer your body any protection from its ultimate fate.

Even Christ had to surrender to the destiny that was on *his* path.

The body is only the smile on the Cheshire Cat of Consciousness. Even after the "person" has vanished, it's just the last thing that disappears.

Your *body* has a destiny.

However, "who you are" does *not* have a destiny.

If you want to stop drinking, it better be scarier for you to be drunk than it is to be sober.

If you're addicted to anything, then you've been worshiping the wrong god.

Instead of surrendering to your Higher Power, you've only been surrendering to the power that gets you *high*.

However, the challenge in life is not to *get* high.

The challenge in life is to *be* high.

J ust as you can understand without accepting, you can also accept without understanding.

Figuring things out first is not a pre-requisite for just embracing things being exactly as they are.

If you won't accept things as they are, can you, at least, accept your non-acceptance of them?

Or, if necessary, can you accept your nonacceptance of your non-acceptance?

Don't try to resist your resistances.

And, don't even resist your resistances to your resistances.

And on and on.

Saying yes to your yeses is easy.

But it's very important that you also say yes to your no's, too.

The universe is always inviting you to let go.

However, if you're unwilling to let things go when it's time for them to go, they'll *still* be taken away from you.

And, sometimes, very roughly.

Learn to let go of what's *already* gone.

Sometimes, it's even easier to let go of things than it is to let go of the persistent belief that "I'm the one who is letting go of these things."

In awakening, you also have to let go of the concept of "letting go."

Then there's only letting go of letting go.

B hakti yoga says, "Surrender to God."

Advaita Vedanta says, "Everything is One."

Consciousness, however, has no comment about *either* position.

No matter your inclination, however, trust that you'll always be shown what you need to be shown and that you'll always be taught what you need to be taught.

Your spiritual path actually chooses *you*, and, sooner or later, its sacred labyrinth will lead you, inexorably, directly into the very Heart of who you are.

But, paradoxically, this longed-for rendezvous with your own Self has *already* taken place.

You already *are* what you are seeking.

Y ou were born to do *exactly* whatever it is that you're, seemingly, doing right now.

Your entire life's purpose is being perfectly and totally fulfilled, every single second.

Things always work out for you—*if* you're willing to give up your idea about what working out looks like.

Working out looks *exactly* like what is, and what is looks exactly like what should be.

Since many things in life just don't make any sense at all, get more comfortable being in the mindless state of not knowing/not understanding.

Have you noticed that trying to work out your karma is a lot like trying to get out of quicksand?

The more that you seemingly do to work it out, the more stuck you seem to become.

Doing only begets still *more* doing.

The actor keeps getting seduced by believing in the ongoing reality of his own act.

The only way to wake up is to discover the one who believes that he is sleeping.

Here's a clue: Know One is here.

DON'T MIND ANYTHING

I'm looking at myself,
reflections of my mind.

—The Moody Blues

Since Being itself has no opposite, dualism is only a construct of the mind—a reflected (and projected) made-up story that Being is telling to itself in order to play.

And our chronic self-absorption plays a big part in the telling, and the re-telling, of that story.

In essence, we're all just worshipping ourselves at the private altar of "me."

And, ironically, we all end up playing both the priest *and* the sacrificial lamb.

The nature of the mind is to keep the screen of Consciousness filled with seductive manifestations.

In short, we all love the razzle-dazzle that comes along with the appearance of The Other.

Above all, your mind doesn't want to get kicked out of the Ego Game too quickly.

It desperately wants to be the last final Survivor.

The Big Cosmic Joke, however, is that the mind is as non-existent as is the very ego that it's been trying so hard to protect.

Ah, isn't it fun to pretend?

You're forgetting that you've forgotten that you're just *pretending* to be separate from everything else.

The Game of Life is played by the non-existent ego trying to expose the non-existent mind in order to achieve a non-existent enlightenment for some non-existent person.

Mind is only an artificial context—a cosmic stage upon which the ego-based actor struts and frets his stuff upon.

And, yes, it's the very *same* stuff that dreams are made of.

I s the world *on* your mind, or is the world really *in* your mind?

Where does your mind go when there are no thoughts?

Where does the world go when you're not thinking about it?

The fiery mind is kept fueled by the constancy of your thinking.

The ego-based "I" thought (as in "I think _____" or "I feel _____") forms the context for the mind to appear in.

The mind, then, forms the context for the entire universe to show up in.

So, what would happen if you ever stopped stoking the cosmic fire?

Would the universe still appear?

Hmmmm. Find out.

Anyone can hear the noise in their mind that's hiding within the silence.

But can you also hear the silence in your heart that's hiding within the noise?

Only in stillness will you discover the quiet in the middle of the chaos.

Only in stillness will you discover the hush in the middle of the rush.

BUT, IS IT REAL?

Outside of God, there is nothing.

—St. Paul

There's one great delusion that lies at the core of all of our suffering: the false belief in the reality of the separation of life and in the subsequent true existence of an *individual* ego.

All fervent attempts to control or to mortify this illusory ego through penance, rituals, and sacrifice, however, will only serve to *intensify* the delusion that this ego is actually very real and that it only needs to be, somehow, subdued, conquered, or destroyed.

J ust because something *exists*, however, it doesn't necessarily mean that it's *real*.

Reality is that which persists in *all* states — waking life, dream life, and in dreamless sleep.

If this is true, then, anything that fundamentally changes *can't* actually be considered as real.

That doesn't mean, of course, that it doesn't *appear* to exist!

Waking, dreaming, and dreamless sleep are not phases of Consciousness.

They're only phases of the *mind*.

Consequently, trying to kill the proverbial coiled snake in the rope is as impossible as is killing the ego in the mind.

Why?

Neither the snake, nor the mind, are really *real*.

When the mind goes out looking for the reality of Consciousness, all that it will ever find is just *more* mind.

Instead, turn around and see *whose* mind is doing all this so-called looking.

Who you *really* are has absolutely no polarity.

Since Consciousness stands in opposition to *nothing*, it creates no real opposite.

Who you *think* you are, however, *does* appear to have an opposite.

The Game begins anew whenever you start pretending again that you don't recognize your own reflection.

When Consciousness becomes *self-conscious* of itself, it appears to show up in the world as a personal ego.

But why does the ego go out looking for a Consciousness that it *already* is? After all, Consciousness isn't lost that it needs to be, somehow, found.

Although the ego is compelled to go out looking, ironically its only real hope of ever surviving is in *not finding*.

BUT, IS IT REAL?

The visible world is manifested by the dance that goes on between your "I" —what you say you are (i.e., the yes-stuff), and your "not-I," —what you say you are not (i.e., the no-stuff).

Unfortunately, the "not-I" can only talk in terms of who you are *not*.

It has no real language for talking in terms of who you really *are*.

PAST-PRESENT-
FUTURE

*Change is an illusion
because we're always at the place
where any future can take us.*

—Alan Watts

I f you believe that you had a past, then you'll also believe that you'll have a future.

In truth, though, who you *really* are didn't have a so-called past, and it certainly won't be having a so-called future.

The past doesn't have a future that it's living into, and the future hasn't had a past that it's living out of.

So you can't really "seize the day," and you can't even seize the moment.

In fact, you've never been able to seize anything at all!

The present moment unfolds upon, and *into,* itself only in this very moment of Now.

And it leaves no tracks pointing in either direction.

The ego can *only* exist in linear time.

The present moment, however, is timeless because it has neither a beginning nor an end.

By believing in a real past and in a real future, though, the ego creates an opening for fear and desire to begin creating their melodramatic mischief.

The ego's worst fear is always of vanishing into the purifying brilliance of the present moment.

To delay this for as long as possible, though, the ego markets itself, *to itself,* as being something very special and unique.

The ego supports its existence by reminiscing about the past or by speculating about the future.

In other words, it's only able to cling to something that's *not* present.

However, since the present is *always* present, the ego can never find a handhold in the here and now.

The momentum from the illusory past meets the infinite potential of the unrealized future and collapses ultimately into the present moment of now.

In short, *all* of what is is always happening right here and right now.

Since nothing is ever incomplete or missing, you're always having a second-by-second rendezvous with your own fully completed destiny.

You are the personification of the very path in life that you're now walking.

You are the human embodiment of *this* present moment of Now.

Yes, you!

Since you're not blaming the future for the present, why, then, are you so quick to blame the past?

The past can only tell you about the past.

The past can't tell you anything about the present moment.

Paradoxically, though, unless you actively partici-pate in fully honoring the present moment, then your so-called future may look a whole lot like your so-called past.

But here's an important point: Just because the past is unreal, it doesn't mean that it never actu-ally happened.

Real or not, though, you still can't change the past. You can only change your *experience* of the past.

But, of course, that change can never happen *in* the past.

That change can only happen in the present.

W hat's more real: the past, the present, or the future?

Well, is a *picture* of yesterday's waterfall more real than today's waterfall?

The past is touchable *only* from the present, and it only exists now as fleeting memory traces in your brain.

The future is also touchable *only* from the present. Tomorrow's waterfall only exists now as today's imaginary fantasy.

The future is not really "in" the future.

The past is not really "in" the past.

This present moment is what is *sourcing* them both, and it's *all* that you'll ever really have.

Luckily, the present is both touchable and available!

And it's always present.

S ince Consciousness shows up only *in* (and as) the present, then only *this* present moment is really real.

In this precious moment, *you* are both the very presence that you're unwrapping, and unravelling, and the presence that is unwrapping (and unraveling) you.

Truly, you are the priceless Gift that Consciousness is giving to Itself.

You're the perfect Trinity: the Gift Giver, the Gift Receiver, and the Gift Itself.

Three-as-One.

Sound familiar?

O ver the years, who you *think* you are will probably change, again and again.

Who you *really* are, however, (the Cosmic Dreamer) will never change.

The Dreamer's dreams do not have either a past or a future attached to any one of them.

Mysteriously, whatever is going to happen has *already* happened.

Mysteriously, whatever has already happened is *going* to happen.

In the world of forms, everything waits its perfect time to manifest itself.

And the perfect (and *only*) time to manifest anything is always Now.

So everything is *always* fully present. 100 percent!

It just doesn't *appear* to be.

The past is only remembered from the present moment.

Likewise, the future is only imagined from the present moment.

It's in *this* present moment that you're living out your day-to-day melodrama on the very cross-hairs of life itself—the here and the now.

This, right now, is truly It.

So you're *not* really on your way to the end of your life, or to the end of your career, or to the end of your relationship, or to the end of your day, or to the end of your thought, or even to the end of your breath.

In fact, you're not on your way to the end of *any-thing*.

You are standing perfectly still.

The world is really moving *through* you, and mysteriously, moving *as* you.

Crucifixion perfectly symbolizes the ongoing dilemma of the ego.

One hand of your ego is seemingly nailed to your memories about the past while your other hand is seemingly nailed to your imaginings about the future.

Although your body feels pain in the present moment, your ego only adds to its own suffering by blindly worshiping at the altars of memory and imagination.

Until you *fully* surrender to the present moment, you'll always feel that you're being crucified.

CHOOSING TO HAVE NO CONTROL

All know the way
but few actually walk it.

—Bodhidharma

Having choices is very different than having control.

You're still responsible for your choices, even though you have no real control over making them.

However, you can always choose to say that you're *not* really responsible for your choices. But, of course, you still are.

You can give away your control, but you can't give away your responsibility.

Learn to get comfortable with your chaos. Since everything changes and everything ends, your default position in life needs to be an enthusiastic YES! to whatever shows up.

Because there's no *not* now, learn to touch each moment softly. Live your life as if you're arriving *and departing* at the very same moment.

Appreciating your life doesn't mean that you have to be enjoying it all the time. Here's your choice: being comfortable or being *authentic*.

Are you crying because you have no control?

What if, instead, you simply decided to *laugh* at the idea of having no control?

Wouldn't you, then, be experiencing the dramas in your life very differently?

But, then again, maybe you don't even have any control over making *that* decision either!

In other words, you may not have any control over deciding that you have no control.

W hen you choose what is to be fully present for you, you're also, indirectly, choosing what isn't to be present for you, too.

If you don't like what's missing from your life (like money, for example), then you need to discover exactly *why* you've chosen for its absence to be present for you.

And you're only adding to your sadness by putting an equal sign between "something is *missing*" and "something is *wrong*."

The key to happiness lies in consciously *choosing* whatever it is that you're already getting.

And, yes, that means choosing even the uncomfortable stuff, too.

In fact, if you don't consciously choose the uncomfortable stuff, you're *still* going to be getting it anyway.

But now you've got *two* problems instead of one:

1. *Not* getting what you want, and

2. *Resisting* the fact that you're getting what you *don't* want.

I n discovering that you have no real control over your choices, your heart will be set free.

However, if you believe that you have even *one* single choice in life, that's enough to keep you fully trapped and into taking the Game very seriously.

There's an old song that says "Freedom's just another word for nothing left to lose."

In truth, though, freedom's just another word for nothing left to *choose*.

Your spiritual journey can only begin when you give up your attachment to the melodramatic story that you've been calling your life.

Detachment doesn't mean, however, that you're uninvolved with the illusory world.

Detachment only means that your involvement with the world is at such a high level that you have *no* demands about what, or how, it's unfolding.

Consequently, whatever happens in your life is always 100 percent OK with you.

The last step, then, is to become detached from your detachment.

Psychological inquiry is about *content*, and it's directed towards solving some problem.

Spiritual inquiry, however, is about *context*, and it's more directed towards discovering *who* has the problem.

SEEDS FOR THE SOUL

From time to time, notice how your periods of great spiritual insights and clarity are often followed by periods of great spiritual doubt and confusion, and that these seemingly opposite states fluctuate randomly back and forth throughout your entire life.

The ever-growing possibility of no-thing-ness will compel you, again and again, to lose your focus. In order to continue your playful pretending, you pull back at the very last moment and sabotage yourself from full awakening.

But, in truth, you're only playing with your Self.

Have you ever watched how a cat first catches, and then seems to carelessly release the same mouse, again and again?

First the cat has it, and then he pretends that he *doesn't* have it. Again and again.

Likewise, *you* seem to have it.

And then, you pretend that you *don't* have it.

But, it's all really OK.

After all, *nobody* wants a good movie to end.

So, are you drawing freely on the blank canvas of your life or are you really only painting by the numbers?

Perhaps your so-called choices don't really change the direction of your life as much as they're only, in a sense, realigning your inner compass.

Although it may *look* like there's been a change in your course heading, perhaps there's still an underlying historical inevitability to absolutely everything that you've ever been deciding.

As they say, "Que sera, sera."

IS TOTAL FREEDOM
EVEN POSSIBLE?

*At the end of the road is freedom.
Until then, patience.*

—Buddha

The people around you and the life events that you're experiencing are the answers that your Soul has created as a response to your Heart's deepest longing for healing, freedom, and true awakening.

Your personal life's drama, no matter *how* traumatic it is or was, is the path that *you*, yourself, have chosen to bring you into full awakening.

To be truly free, you need to rid yourself of only three things: 1) the desire to *have*, 2) the fear to *lose*, and 3) the need to *change*.

Suffering finds its roots in your desire to be free from something that's either present for you right now or something that you fear *may* be present for you in the future.

Things just seem to change a lot easier whenever we don't make them wrong for being there.

As they say, "resistance is futile."

Your suffering is directly proportional to the intensity of your attachments to these passing phenomena and to the strength of your habit of seeking for some kind of personal identity in the world of forms.

In order to be free from your attachments, you have to be willing to detach yourself from your *attachment* to your attachments.

You can do this only by consciously surrendering to what's so for you, moment to moment to moment.

Giving *in* to what is, is very different than giving *up* on what is.

There's never any reason to celebrate how you could be, or, especially, how you should be.

Your Cosmic celebration of life can only take place around how you really *are*.

F reedom *of* choice seems to be there until freedom *from* choice becomes fully recognized.

In the long run, there's really only nothing to choose.

And nothing can be chosen *only* when there's nobody really there to be choosing it.

Long before "you" showed up, all of the final decisions in your life had *already* been made.

However, the fun part of the Game comes in pretending that this isn't really true.

Although your so-called free will choices seemingly unfold in linear time, the ultimate outcome of all of these decisions has always been *absolutely certain.*

In other words, you're living your life out *into* what you've *already* chosen to experience.

Conveniently, though, you've just forgotten what you've signed up for.

What will ultimately set you free is not freedom from your *body* but freedom from your illusory *mind* and from your belief in your sense of personal do-ership.

Actually, you are not really the do-er of the do-ing.

You're really the *non*-doer of the non-doing.

True freedom is *not* found by freeing yourself *from* experiencing something.

True freedom is only found by freeing yourself *to* experience *everything*.

F reedom: loving it the way that it *is and* loving it the way that it *isn't*.

If all that there is, however, is the Path, then absolutely everything that you find along your way is a part of that Path, too.

There are no mistakes to make, or detours to take. You cannot get off your Path, even if you would want to.

By leading you nowhere, it leads you now-here.

Absolute freedom lies in welcoming everything that shows up on your Path and saying, in effect—

I One It All!

The bad news: You can't really save anyone from their destiny.

In fact, you can't save them even if it's *your* destiny to be involved in *their* destiny.

Period!

The good news, though, is that no one is *ever* going to be damned. Not ever.

No matter what's been happening in your life, you're not being punished.

You're only being taught.

But some Paths can be deceptive.

Watch out for pseudo-spiritual practices that will only make you *high*, but won't make you *free*.

CONSCIOUSNESS— WHO NEEDS IT?

Thou art the seer of thyself.

—Srimad Bhagavatam

Consciousness can handle your life without you and your controlling ego ever being involved.

The movie screen has no need to control the characters that are appearing in the movie.

The screen of Consciousness equally accepts every comedy, melodrama, farce, and tragedy, without *any* discrimination whatsoever.

Consciousness is even big enough to welcome your perversions and to tolerate your holiness.

It's only you who seem to have a problem in *equally* embracing all of these passing phenomena.

Consciousness isn't really pure or impure.

It just Is-What-It-Is.

Because they're always making so many value judgments, the ego and the mind invariably become *problems* for both the ego and the mind.

The ego and the mind, however, are never a problem for Consciousness.

By identifying new polarities, the judgmental ego, though, always has new positions to cling to.

Since Consciousness contains *all* polarities, however, it refuses to take *any* stand at all.

Consequently, the ego always wants to run the other way.

The screen of Consciousness itself is absolutely still and completely unmoved by any of the images that are being projected upon it.

The joy of awakening might lie in discovering who you already are (i.e. the Screen), but the real *fun* might lie in continuing to pretend that you're still caught up in the storyline of your drama.

After all, even the Screen might want to enjoy the movie!

You create your cosmic Play by casting it with make-believe others who will help you to awaken from your persistent illusion of separation.

But the God that you're seeking is *neither* inside you nor is it outside you.

There can be no boundaries around God simply because there's *only* God.

No-thing else. No one else.

Period. The End.

And so, no spiritual teacher should ever claim to be doing God's work.

God doesn't work. God only plays.

It just sometimes *looks* like work.

So maybe we need more teachers who are willing to do God's *play*.

From the stream of Consciousness, the ego filter catches the world by drawing imaginary boundaries, and then claims personal ownership of the thoughts, feelings, words, and actions that show up.

But when you find the courage to take *off* the "no" filter, then everything that shows up becomes magically OK.

Then there's no position to be fighting for, and there's no position to be resisting against.

Then there's only an unbroken and seamless Consciousness.

But, it's a Consciousness without any content.

It's just pure awareness.

But an awareness that doesn't have anything to be aware of.

You can't turn either towards Consciousness or away from Consciousness.

In fact, you can't even turn at all because your life is really only a melodramatic story that Consciousness has been telling to Itself.

And your only choice is whether or not you want to believe in the validity of your story.

As usual, the ego wants to proudly say, "That's *my* story, and I'm sticking to it."

Actually, since you and your story arise simultaneously, your story is also sticking to *you*!

Without the historical framework of your time-based story, though, "you" are really "no-thing."

Actually, being no-thing might not be such a bad idea.

L ike the movie screen, Consciousness pretends to both *be* something and to *not* be something at the very same time.

For example, Consciousness pretends to be the table. However, at the very same time, Consciousness is also pretending to not be that very same table, too.

The table can't even appear unless Consciousness *equally* pretends that it's *also* the empty space that the table is now appearing in and is surrounded by.

However, Consciousness is always neutral and has absolutely *no* attachment whatsoever to either the table or to the space that's around the table.

Consciousness is able to play *all* opposing sides, *simultaneously*.

Consequently, it's not interested in any of the ego-based distinctions of either-or.

Since it's able to contain *all* opposites, Consciousness does not (and *can* not) ever take a firm position on anything.

Only the ego wants to take a firm position.

Unlike all of the "gods," though, Consciousness doesn't take sides.

C onsciousness is always doing business as *something* by creating over here and destroying over there.

But all conflict is only illusory because every opposite position is also that very same Consciousness, too.

Since it's all only *you*, you've only been tilting at the windmills in your mind.

Consequently, there's *nothing* in life that's *not* spiritual because there's *nothing* in life that's *not* Consciousness.

Give up your idea about what spirituality looks like.

Spirituality looks *exactly* like what is.

In order to seemingly pre-date the body, Consciousness fashions an elaborate historically-based context that perfectly supports the cosmic pretense.

You were, for example, told that you were born on a certain calendar date, and that you were the latest addition in a long line of living adults and dead ancestors.

The inertia created by fear and desire, then, propels your storyline out into this make believe world in order to begin dancing the proverbial Dance of the Divine.

However, *this* Dance requires that you initially wear the mask of a personalized ego.

In order to see himself in a mirror, however, the Invisible Man had to also wear a mask.

For you, though, the Great Discovery is that the entire world is your masking.

G reat teachers and philosophies are like special portals that point you into the infinite vastness of Consciousness.

However, most Seekers get stuck at these doorways whenever they begin to worship the portal itself instead of looking into what they're being pointed towards.

Unless you find the inner courage to eventually walk through these Gateways, and be *destroyed*, you'll spend your life teetering at the edge of your own emptiness.

Stop seeking outside of you for something that only lies within.

Portals are *not* the Truth.

Portals only point *out* the Truth.

But be still. Be patient.

Sooner or later, all roads lead to Om.

No matter how extreme they might be, all polarities are equally supported by the unconditional yes of Consciousness.

Since it's so totally in love with Itself, Consciousness is always saying yes to absolutely everything that life presents to It.

In fact, Consciousness will *only* say no if you ever ask it to *stop* saying yes.

In a sense, you are a Prime Number.

A Prime Number is a number that can only be divided by one and by itself.

If you try to divide yourself by One, you'll still end up with just yourself.

However, if you divide yourself *by yourself*, then you'll suddenly end up as One.

The truth is revealed only when you're willing to always stay fully divisible by your *entire* truth, moment to moment.

If you leave *anything* out, however, you won't awaken.

The center of the Cosmos lies in the center of your own heart.

A trillion times a second, you're both creating, and destroying, the entire universe.

So of what is there to be afraid?

Is a Mother ever afraid of her own infant?

At every moment, you are *already* cradling your Beloved.

Even as you, yourself, are being cradled.

CAN YOU EVER BE HAPPY?

*People are about as happy
as they want to be.*

—Abraham Lincoln

Our contentment in life does not depend on the *content* that shows up in it.

Our contentment depends only on our willingness to hold the content of our life within a context that is absolutely limitless.

Happiness will always be present for you whenever you become willing to allow the *experience* of happiness to come and go as it pleases.

Obviously, you're happy when you're happy, but the *real* secret of happiness lies in also being willing to be happy when you're *unhappy*.

If you try to cling desperately to your fleeting moments of *happiness*, they'll tend to disappear much quicker.

Likewise, if you openly resist your moments of *unhappiness*, they'll tend to hang around you much longer.

Learn to float freely on the Ocean of Emotion.

Up and down. Up and down.

Your happiness is ultimately determined by whether or not it's OK with you that you're getting what you're getting, whatever that might be.

Unhappiness is only the ego-mind insisting that this should *not* be so.

True happiness of the heart, however, always lies in not "minding" *anything*.

H appiness is learning how to be OK with the world.

Joy is learning how to be OK with your *Self*.

Peace is learning how to be OK with just *be*-ing.

Joy is total peace, while in *motion*.

Peace is total joy, while at *rest*.

If you're not 100 percent happy in the present moment of Now, then you'll unconsciously create reasons for you to seek happiness out in some imaginary future where you can, hopefully, become satisfied, sanctified, or made more whole.

However, if you believe that true happiness is just around the corner for you, you'll always be noticing more corners.

B ecause it never changes, Consciousness itself is never angry, sad, hurt, lonely, or scared.

It's only the historical ego-self that seeks to validate its separate existence by maintaining a close association with, and attachment *for*, these thoughts and feelings.

When you create a heart-centered detachment to the world, however, these passing phenomena can then be experienced with compassionate in-difference and a kind of holy apathy.

Detachment is the realm of unconditional love.

Your happiness depends primarily on your capacity, and your willingness, to fully express the perfect love that you are.

The real secret of permanent happiness lies in not *no*-ing anything.

In short, don't *no* who, or how, you are.

Instead, *be* who you are.

To know the One, you have to be willing to *no* the two.

Paradoxically, though, there's really nothing out there to *no* at all.

The One cannot *no* itself.

It can only *be* itself.

STINKING
THINKING?

We are what we think,
having become what we thought.

—The Dhammapada

You don't need to think in order to exist.

After all, while you were in deep sleep, didn't you still continue to exist without thinking?

Thoughts and feelings appear to arise and fall only within the context of your awareness of them.

The problems begin when you try to take the credit (or the blame) for how these phenomena are showing up for you.

In truth, though, who you really are has absolutely nothing to do with any of them.

Awareness is the context in which ego arises, and the ego is the context in which thought arises.

The fiery mind is constantly fueled by your un-ending thoughts.

However the Witness of a thought is no more its owner than the screen is the owner of the movie characters that are being projected upon it.

When you begin to objectively witness your thoughts coming and going of their own accord, then you'll stop stoking the fire.

Look at them all, *but don't touch.*

The thoughts and feelings appear to be very real.

However, what's *not* real is "you" actually being the Thinker and the Feeler.

Consciousness is really doing it all, and its first thought is always "I am."

Its second thought, however, is always "I am something-or-other."

What creates the you-niverse, and all the mischief, is always its *second* thought.

The "I" thought creates a necessary context for the mind to appear in.

The mind, then, forms the context for the world to appear in.

But where does mind go when there are no thoughts to be thought?

Where does the world go when you're not thinking about the world?

Maybe, in fact, the universe only thinks about *you* in order to have *you* think it into existence.

Thoughts are like soap bubbles—and with about as much real substance.

They're shiny and attractive, but they're also transitory and they encapsulate nothing.

In fact, if looked for, you cannot actually find a thought anywhere.

So, can you ever learn to become completely thought-less?

Since you are *not* your thoughts, there's no reason to be afraid of not thinking.

After all, a car doesn't always have to be in gear in order for the engine to be running.

E ven in awakening, though, the thinking doesn't stop.

What *does* stop, however, is the belief that you are the prime thinker of the thoughts.

In other words, the existence of the "I" is not the real delusion.

The delusion is in believing that the "I" is real, and that this "I" is, somehow, fully capable of originating its thought *by itself*.

EGO, EGO, WE ALL GO FOR EGO

*We are like one in water crying out
"I thirst!"*

—Zen Master Hakuin

The personified interface between what you think you *are* (the I) and what you think you are *not* (the not-I) is the realm of the ego.

But the ego can exist only in linear time.

Without a remembered past or an imagined future, the ego's time-based storyline has absolutely nothing to cling to.

Its special status quickly diminishes in the brilliance of the Eternal Present.

The most problematic paradigm in life is the false belief that there's really a separate, personified you, and that this you is, somehow, moving along through space and time and out into some manifested world.

In fact, though, you are really an oddball collection of various and ever-changing points of view, all apparently radiating outward from some empty and hollow ego center.

And in the very Heart of that ego center no *separate* one is there.

But, quite paradoxically, absolutely *everyone* is there.

B y overlaying a subjective grid work on the world through your definitions and beliefs, you vainly try to artificially divide the indivisible.

Beneath all of your ego-based interpretations, however, the Absolute persists undisturbed and is completely untouched by everything that you think, feel, say, and do.

Meanwhile, though, you're still struggling to frantically write the story of your life on the watery surface of an Eternal Ocean.

But you're using an icicle pen!

You are a clustering of ever-changing points of view whirling around a place whose center is nowhere and whose circumference is everywhere.

The dualities of life radiate out in all directions from the point of view that you *think* that you are.

Without your ongoing interpretations of them, however, these polarities simply collapse down into no-thing-ness.

Amazingly, maybe it's only your ego-based definitions and beliefs about the universe that actually keep everything from *im*ploding.

E veryone has only one *real* mission in life—to awaken from the delusion that they're separate from everything else.

In fact, this persistent delusion is the root cause of most of your emotional and physical problems.

Your present life's condition at this very moment is your Soul's current answer to its #1 question:

"What has to happen right now in order for me to wake up to who I am?"

The answer is always "Whatever *is* happening right now."

In life, there's no *separate* one to leave behind, and there's no separate one who's ever doing the leaving.

This is the absolute truth.

Nobody's coming, and nobody's going.

Amazingly, there's also no separate one who's actually written these words, and there's no separate one who's actually reading them.

No one.

Yes. Know One.

(Go figure.)

The ego thrives on conflict.

It stokes its drama by enthusiastically ref-ereeing the ongoing struggle between this and that.

And the ego always runs away from what is.

If the not-I is real, the ego assumes, then the I has to *also* be real.

However, spiritual victory lies in discovering that there's absolutely no one out there for you to be going to war with.

The scary shadows that you've been fighting with have all been of your *own* making.

That there is a devil, there can be no doubt. But is he trying to get *in* us, or trying to get *out?*

When you're resisting what is, then you're unable to celebrate the present moment of *now*.

What shows up for you instead, then, is either fear or desire that what is will soon be changing into something else.

Resistance to life only reinforces arbitrary boundaries and serves to feed into the separation delusion of the insatiable ego.

But, in truth, there are no *real* boundaries anywhere in life.

That's right. Absolutely no boundaries!

There are, however, a lot of distinctions.

Distinctions, however, don't create any *friction*.

Only boundaries tend to create friction.

And friction is *exactly* why the ego likes to create boundaries so much.

U roborus is the name of the symbolic snake that cannibalistically swallows its own tail.

Likewise, your teachers and their teachings are only reflections and projections of yourself.

Learn to sacramentally swallow them all.

Don't say no to anything.

Above all, you must especially learn to swallow your long standing belief that there's an *unen-lightened* you that's slowly becoming more and more enlightened.

But don't chew on all of this too much.

Instead, learn to swallow.

All judging of others creates an implied hierarchy into which a personal you struggles to fit in.

Discrimination, however, is simply *noticing* the apparent distinctions between things without adding anything else to your observations.

In the end, though, absolutely *everything* must be welcomed by you with an open and non-resistant heart.

Heaven and Earth are separated *only* by the differences, no matter how slight, that you see between what is and what you think should be instead.

High self-esteem and low self-esteem are just different sides of the same coin.

They each assume that there's a *separate* and independent self that's feeling, or that's not feeling, a certain level of esteem about itself.

Both positions *equally* support the illusion of the actual existence of a real coin, a real historical self.

In true awakening, though, there can be no coinage.

The bad news is that your ego will eventually be totally destroyed.

However, the good news is that it never really existed anyway.

Your mind is the only thing standing between your ego and its final annihilation.

The Big Joke, however, is that the so-called mind is as unreal as is the very ego that it is trying to protect!

The mind is an illusion that's protecting an illusion that's protecting an illusion…

And on and on.

The ego maintains its separation from the world by filling the emptiness of emptiness with the emptiness of *form*.

It's obvious that emptiness can always be filled with form, but the *real* awakening comes in discovering that form can *also* be filled with emptiness.

The ego, however, is just not too interested in learning about that.

The ego survives by trying to pretend that *it* is the thinker, feeler, speaker and do-er.

These phenomena serve as the handholds for the ego to seemingly survive within the vast emptiness of Consciousness.

But if you're ever to live as who you *really* are, you must first die completely to who you *think* you are.

The final annihilation is *not* of your self.

The final annihilation is of your *story*.

Memories about the past ("I was_____") and imaginings about the future ("I will_____") are the ongoing story that you're telling yourself in order to support your ego's sense of personal do-ership.

Such persistent thoughts, though, are only the poles that you're using to prop up the tent of your empty ego.

The mischief begins again whenever you start to believe *everything* that you think.

But, since you're not the *real* Thinker, maybe you shouldn't be believing *anything* that you think.

What isn't doesn't really *oppose* what is, just like how no doesn't really *oppose* yes.

Only the ego sets up opposition to yes by taking the side, and the form, of no.

The ego's survival depends on maintaining its belief that it (and it alone) is the experiencer of the experience.

Actually, though, only Consciousness is really experiencing it all.

The body is just along for the ride.

LET'S PRETEND

*It is all only a great game
of pretending.*

—Ramana Maharshi

I t's your nature to be what you are by *pretending* to become what you're pretending to *not* be.

The visible world that you experience is only the physical manifestation of the things inside you that you're pretending to *not* be.

No matter what else the world seems to be, it's all only a reflection of *you*.

You're not living *on* the world, and you're not living *in* the world.

You're always living *as* the world.

The parts of the universe that you don't *fully* absorb become the mask of your persona that then gets projected out to the world as who you are.

So, consequently, you are a part of who, and what, I'm pretending that I'm *not*.

And, of course, vice versa.

Deep down, you are what you've always suspected that you are:

The Great Pretender.

The only way that the Infinite can express the love that it has for Itself is by pretending to become what it isn't.

In other words, finite.

You create the physical world when you identify yourself more with what you're pretending to be than you do when you identify yourself with what you're pretending to *not* be.

The infinite *loves* to play at being finite.

In the end, though, it only wants to free-fall into the love that It already is.

T he Game is played by simply forgetting that you've forgotten that you're just *pretending* to be separate.

As long as you continue to pretend that you're either getting it or losing it, then you can also continue to pretend that you're not really Be-ing it.

So play as though you really don't *know* that you're only playing.

Play as though all of it really matters—even though it really doesn't matter.

In fact, play as though it doesn't even matter that it doesn't even matter.

You are not a part of God nor is God a part of you.

By definition, God can't have any parts.

God can only *pretend* to have parts.

You—as the historical ego-self—are one of these so-called parts that God is pretending to have.

W ho you *really* are has never actually moved at all.

In fact, you are in the *exact* same spot where you were born, where you went to school, had your first date, became successful, experienced your many adventures and finally got to be as old as you are.

And, you're already at the exact spot where you are, apparently, going to die.

So, *who* are you?

Are you one of the images being projected onto the cosmic Screen, or are you really the entire Screen itself that's *pretending* to be only one of the images?

And, of course, what happens when you just *stop* pretending?

Maybe the movie's not over just because you discover that it's only a movie.

Maybe all of your choices have already been chosen.

And maybe you're just pretending that you haven't really chosen them yet.

In fact, maybe you're only choosing to pretend that you even *have* any so-called choices at all to begin with.

But, if that's true, can you even choose to control that you're only pretending that you can even choose *anything* in the first place?

One more question: Can you even choose to *not* think about any of this?

You are spirit-being pretending to be human-becoming.

In order to play out its drama, though, Consciousness seduces itself by *pretending* to be unconscious.

When Consciousness pretends to be and to not be—at the very same time—then the world magically appears.

So part of your playing at life lies in pretending that life is *not* a play.

In short, you're really pretending that you're *not* pretending.

In other words, you're *waking* yourself up by *making* yourself up.

To support your sense of do-ership, though, you pretend that you *haven't* chosen 100 percent of what you're experiencing.

But, if the decisions may have already been made, then your so-called choices will always lead you into experiencing whatever it is that you've already decided to experience.

You can't escape from what you've signed up for.

Is it possible that we unconsciously hurt ourselves because we inwardly know that our deepest pain can often trigger Grace?

Do we, perhaps, deliberately seek out pain and pleasure in order to more fully participate in the extremes of experience that are available in this human incarnation?

So, no matter what shows up for it, Consciousness is always saying yes to absolutely everything, no matter *how* radical or off-the-wall it might be.

Consciousness is an Experience Junkie!

Consciousness is a single party of One—trying to have a wild party as Two.

It only wants to feast on the Feast.

Since we're all pre-death, no one is going to get out alive.

We're all on Death Row.

But there's nothing to worry about because death won't, and *can't*, kill you.

After all, what was never really born can never really die.

The final freedom lies in discovering that your jail cell has never been locked.

The unknown always creates its power by making itself scarier than the known.

Worrying about the future, though, is always a waste of time.

Why pay the rent before the rent is due?

The cosmic irony: The part of you that creates your problems is the exact *same* part of you that you call upon to *solve* these same problems.

Since who you really are is never a problem, it should take absolutely *no* effort for you to simply relax and *be* who you already are.

In fact, it actually takes a lot more effort to try to be who you are *not*.

So maybe it's best to stop making so much effort, and just be.

Saying that *I'm* not the do-er of the action quietly implies that someone *else* is the do-er.

But, in Truth, there's nothing that's being done,
and there's no separate one out there who's really doing it, anyway.

As soon as it *appears* that things are being done,
then, sooner or later, someone is going to be taking the credit, or the blame.

But why be *some* one when you can be *no* one?

Why be *some* where when you can be *every*
where?

Why be *some* thing when you can be *no* thing?

You create your dualistic world when you identify more with what you're pretending to *be* than you do when you identify with what you're pretending to *not* be.

In this dualistic world, you're always defined by the beliefs about it that you create.

The big trick is to fully *commit* yourself to all of your beliefs, but without becoming attached to *any* of them.

Remember—*in* the world, but not *of* it.

An actor on stage who *knows* that he's only pretending will have a very different experience of the drama than a fellow actor who is *so* much into his character that he's completely forgotten that he's only pretending.

From the audience's point of view, however, both of these actors will appear to be totally involved in the play.

Even though they *both* exist as characters in the production, *one* of them will enjoy the playfulness that underlies the melodrama while the other one will believe that he is personally suffering the consequences that flow from the decisions that are made by his character.

In short, since he doesn't remember that he's *only* playing a role, he'll believe that it's all really happening to him!

WHAT IS ILLUSORY?

*All that we see or seem
is but a dream within a dream.*

—Edgar Allan Poe

The world is not the illusion.

It's *you* who are the illusion.

Who you are is the context that the entire world is happening in.

As long as you are in the body, however, you won't be waking up *from* the illusion.

You'll only be waking up *to* the illusion.

Even after you've discovered that it's only illusory, the mirage of a desert lake *still* looks just like a real lake.

When you don't recognize the world as yourself, you'll always be entranced by seeing your own unrecognized reflection.

The reflected image and the unblemished mirror appear to arise simultaneously.

Without the mirror, though, the reflected image is invisible.

Likewise, without the reflected image, the mirror is equally invisible.

It's the same with you and the world.

As cosmic co-conspirators, you appear, and you disappear, simultaneously.

When you stop pretending and fall asleep, you withdraw the entire world into your heart just like the spider withdraws its web into its own body.

Then, when you awaken again, you spontaneously recreate the web of life and get quickly ensnared by the irresistible seductiveness of your own reflection.

The fear-and-desire diversions that immediately arise cleverly distract you from remembering the Truth of who you really are.

But *then*, of course, you're better able to play out into the wonders of your wonderland.

Sleeping again, though, you once more become the destroyer of worlds.

You don't sing a song in order to arrive at the final note.

The joy of a song is always in the *singing* of it.

It's the same thing with life.

The joy of life is in the *living* of it.

The Dance of the Divine is fully honored whenever the Dancer *really* dances the dance!

So, start dancing—right where you are!

As strange as it sounds, the population of the entire world is only *one*.

So, when *you* are taking a bath, the whole world is actually taking a bath.

In fact, whatever you're doing right now this very second is the *only* thing that the universe is really doing.

You're just pretending that this isn't so by creating time (past and future), space (here and there), and the belief that you're a separate person living in a world filled with other separate people (I and not-I).

Consciousness *loves* to divide the indivisible.

A hungry dreamer can only be satisfied by eating dream food.

Likewise, a hungry spirit can only be satisfied by eating spiritual food.

Here's another taste:

You're living in paradise the very moment that you *completely* give up your hidden demands about what paradise should be looking like.

Paradise doesn't look like what isn't.

Paradise always looks *exactly* like what is.

The personification of Consciousness (the ego) arises because it's unwilling to die to its dream of having an individual person-hood.

But just like there can be light without heat, there can also be personality without there being a *separate* person.

Dream characters (including the dreamed version of you) all vanish in the morning light.

In final awakening, however, your person-hood will *also* have to vanish.

A good therapist will help you to *grow up* and to create *better* dreams.

A satguru, however, will help you to *wake up* and to stop dreaming altogether.

A red apple is not really red.

It's actually *reflecting* red while absorbing all of the other colors.

Likewise, every object in the universe also contains every other object.

Every other object, that is, except *itself*.

Non-absorbed vibrations, much like the red in the apple, get reflected outward and serve to create the manifested universe.

This is true for you, too.

After absorbing the *entire* universe, what's reflected outward as your persona is then falsely perceived as being who you are.

I am whatever it is that you are pretending to *not* be.

And, of course, vice versa.

You come in many disguises, and I am wearing one of them.

A good question: "Was I always _____?" (insert your name)

A better (and far deeper) question might be:

"Was I *ever* _____?" (insert your name)

As expected, the true inquiry is always *within*.

ENLIGHTENMENT— ARE WE THERE YET?

*The one you are looking for
is the same one
who is doing the looking.*

—St. Francis of Assisi

If you believe that you are unenlightened, your mind will be *compelled* to create life experiences and conditions for you that you'll come to view as life experiences and conditions that happen to someone who is unenlightened.

If you argue for your spiritual limitations, you will always win.

The energizing dynamic for the entire cosmos lies in its relentlessly seeking for reunion with the mysterious other, the not-I.

The great melodramas of Life, however, are recreated, again and again, whenever the cosmos secretly *sabotages* this longed-for union from ever taking place.

Your spiritual labyrinth first leads you towards, and then away from, the center of the Heart.

Over and over.

B ecause the mind is not real, it can *never* become enlightened.

Wanting desperately to survive, however, the mind tries to pass itself off as real by implying that it's *who* you are.

Although it *says* it wants to wake up to itself, the mind will delay for as long as possible its own inevitable exposure as a non-existent phantom.

Even illusions don't want to voluntarily end their illusory status.

W hen you're asleep and truly *know* that you're dreaming, it's called lucid dreaming.

However, when you're awake and *still* know that you're dreaming, then it's called enlightenment.

Right now, you're not really awake.

You're only *dreaming* that you're awake.

And, ironically, a big part of that dream is that, someday, you will eventually awaken.

The proverbial Gateway to Enlightenment is seemingly guarded by two fierce Demons of the Mind: Paradox and Confusion.

For example, the more that you run after enlightenment, no matter *how* sincerely, the more that it will seem to flee before you.

Struggling to be enlightened only reinforces your illusion of separation, which then, of course, only encourages you to struggle even more.

And on. And on. And on.

The hidden secret about enlightenment is that you can't get *there* from here.

You can only get *here* from here.

The biggest obstacles to enlightenment are your *desire* to personally *witness* and *survive* that radical awakening, and your inner fear that you simply won't be able to.

But don't worry about losing your personal identity in the One-ness.

Others will mysteriously show up in your life who will carry that heavy burden for you by telling you who they see you to be.

That doesn't mean, of course, that *that's* who you really are.

There are never any guaranteed pathways to enlightenment.

However, you'll still be compelled to walk some of them anyway until you're finally convinced that, in the end, they'll *all* have to be abandoned, too.

The great awakening lies in discovering that, all along, you've only been marching in place.

And then, you just stop marching.

And stay perfectly still.

And surrender to your Self.

H alf of being enlightened lies in knowing in your heart of hearts that there's no *separate* one really there who's going to be enlightened.

The other half is Grace.

Enlightenment is *not* something that you can ever learn, or earn.

It's only something that you can, perhaps, *discover*.

The great paradox, however, is that there's no separate one there at all who can even make this discovery.

The Original Sin is in believing in the separate reality of an Original Sinner.

Enlightenment is not about knowing *some* thing.

Enlightenment is about *being* no-thing.

There are *no* spiritual levels to achieve before you're finally awarded with an official Graduation Certificate of Enlightenment.

Enlightenment is not about winning some cosmic Game.

Since you're simultaneously playing *all* of the many sides of life, you're both winning and losing, at the very same time.

Enlightenment is only about piercing the Grand Illusion itself and discovering that, deep down, you already *are* the entire Game of life itself.

Transcending *this* dream, however, first necessitates trance-*ending*.

S ooner or later, you will realize that you already *are* who your Heart has been looking for.

Since you can't become any *more* of who you *already* are, your search will eventually end right where it had originally begun: with your *Self*.

But, if you don't recognize that your inner quest has come full circle, you'll likely set off on yet another outward quest, hoping that a dualistic world view will, somehow, trigger your awakening.

Ten Steps to Spiritual Evolution:

Dream up. Show up. Grow up. Gather up. Build up. Screw up. Blow up. Lighten up. Give up.

Wake up.

G ive up waiting for the proverbial Enlightenment Bus to come along for you.

It's *never* going to show up.

Not ever!

Who you *really* are will never—and *can* never—get enlightened.

Getting enlightened is not a big task for who you *are*.

Getting enlightened is only a big task for who you are *not*.

You won't find what you're looking for until you first discover *who* is the one who is doing all of this so-called looking.

When the I goes seeking for the source of the I thought, it's a lot like trying to boot up a heart-based computer.

In *this* awakening, though, the God that you've been searching for is discovered to be *both* immanent *and* transcendent.

God is (t)here.

But, in truth, there's really *Nothing* between you and God.

Not ever.

(Even if you say that there is.)

E nlightenment reframes everything so that *nothing* is framed.

There's content, but there's never a *final* context that it can all be held in.

In enlightenment, the content of life itself becomes its very *own* context.

In the end, the same infinite Source always ends up sourcing it all.

And, quite mysteriously, that same Source even sources *itself*.

Don't ask the Saints about enlightenment.

One question only leads to another.

And, after all, not even God can explain God.

Besides, a saint isn't any closer to enlightenment than is a sinner.

The only difference between them is that a saint *knows* this while the sinner is still *pretending* that he doesn't.

The Heart of Enlightenment lies in discovering that we're *all* living in the very heart center of each other!

Y ou are not a Divine Being.

You are actually *the* Divine—*Be*-ing.

When you wake up, you can't simply substitute one dream called Once I Was Asleep for a *newer* dream called But *Now* I Am Awake.

The dreaming god must first awaken to his own dreaming.

But there are not *two* different gods here—one who is so-called sleeping and another one who is so-called awake.

Paradoxically, the god who says that he is asleep is also the very *same* god who is now saying that he is awake.

Simply put, you are The One.

But, you're pretending to be two.

So then you start to desperately seek for a reunion with The One.

The incredible irony is that it's a One which you *already* are and have never stopped being.

A dog chasing its own tail will only get dizzy and an occasional mouthful of hair.

But in Enlightenment, there's really no further chasing of *anything*.

Only, perhaps, a deepening.

Enlightenment is simply being willing to dance joyously, and with total gratitude, to *whatever* music that's being played for you, moment to moment.

After all, it's *all* for your benefit.

Just don't sit out the Dance!

Saying "I am God!" is really the height of spiritual solipsism.

The statement leaves out a very simple but very important little word: is.

The truth is that "I am—*is* God."

You, the historical ego-self, aren't even really here at all.

Only God is here.

In fact, it's really *all* go(o)d.

The simplicity of God is so absolute that God can *only* manifest by *pretending* to be incredibly complex.

Part of that pretended complexity is to create a lot of value-judgments about things, especially about Itself.

For example, it shows up when you believe that "An Enlightened Being wouldn't behave like *I* do!"

But how can you really be so sure?

Isn't it God's very nature to be, basically, unfigure-out-able?

The finite will *never* understand the infinite.

If it did, it would have to give up all of its finiteness, and it's certainly *not* willing to do *that*.

No matter what it says, the thimble really doesn't want to be filled with the ocean.

You don't have to live in a mountain cave and meditate for thirty years.

You can wake up spiritually right now in the middle of the busiest marketplace.

Beneath all of the chaos that's around you, lies the Silence that's within you.

But you don't have to avoid the rush of life.

If you can't get *out* of it, then get further *into* it.

Use the rush—to get into the hush!

A nd so, over and over, life continues to unfold and occasionally, unravel, in wondrous ways.

Even when it appears to be doubling back upon itself, life only presents to you, again and again, what always was (and is) from the very beginning: your very own self!

You can't find your special treasure—either within or without—simply because it's *all* treasure!

And *that's* the Great Secret:

All there *is*, is treasure!

Right now, this very moment, you're sitting in your very own Treasure House!

You already *are* the very treasure that you've been seeking!

So, treasure your Self.

And, of course, dance!

ALL ABOUT NOTHING

Nothing is *very* important.

In fact, *nothing* really matters simply because there's *nothing* going on. There's nothing to be afraid of, and there's nothing to worry about.

There's nothing to learn, nothing to remember, nothing to build on, nothing to save, nothing to hang onto, and nothing to let go of.

While nothing will be able to move you, nothing will ultimately satisfy you. Nothing is going to work out, and there's really nothing to look forward to.

Nothing will make you angry, and nothing can hurt you. Nothing will make you succeed, and nothing will make you fail.

Nothing is happening right now and yet, in the end, nothing will ever change.

Amazingly, nothing has been named.

Ironically, its name is *every* name.

EPILOGUE—WISDOM IN THE ROUND

The Truth of who you really are is often hiding in plain sight.

The cosmic clues are everywhere: in music, books, paintings, movies, poems, songs, plays, sculpture, photographs, etc.

Your very best clues, though, are sometimes hidden in the unlikeliest of places.

For example, do you think that you could ever write something that would be the perfect expression of the greatest wisdom—the very quintessential core of Reality itself? Then, in that same description, could you *also* include the most practical way of living out your day-to-day existence in the light of such an awesome Truth?

One more condition: Could you then limit your summary of these profound teachings, both spiritual and psychological, to only eighteen common words?

That's right: only eighteen simple words!

Give up? Well, relax because someone else has already done it for you. In fact, you already know these eighteen words because they've been a part of your American heritage since you were very young.

Remember some of the campfire songs that you used to sing as a round? One of the old classics was "Row, row, row your boat."

Well, I contend that this simple little ditty describes not only the ultimate Truth of the Universe, but that it also gives very practical advice about how to live your life out in the face of that Reality.

For those of you raised in another country, the words to this little campfire song go like this:

"Row, row, row your boat,
Gently down the stream,
Merrily, merrily, merrily, merrily,
Life is but a dream."

In the very first line, the song implies that you're making some kind of journey over water in "your boat." Most importantly, however, the line begins by repeating the very same action word (row, row, row...) three times, reminding you that, on this journey, you'll need to be expending energy, persistence, and ongoing effort.

In the second line, however, the song implies that you also shouldn't be pushing the river. Instead, it suggests that you should be performing all of this rowing activity very *gently*. Not with anger or resistance or by using brute force, but gently, which means (according to the dictionary), with ease, grace, and with both courtesy and kindness.

The second part of the line reminds you that, while you're gently rowing along, your boat is *still* headed in a particular direction, specifically *down*-stream. It doesn't suggest that you could go against the current or even across it. Instead, the line implies that inexorably (and, like it or not) your boat is still going "*down* the stream."

And, since it's carrying you along some predetermined route (the streambed itself), there's no reason to struggle against where it's taking you. So, the first two lines of the song suggest that you need to make an ongoing effort on your own behalf ("row, row, row"), but on the other hand, you also need to be willing to surrender to the whole inevitability of the process.

The third line is the key: it tells you not only *how* you should perform all of this rowing, but *what* you should be feeling in your heart while you're doing it. The song suggests, quite frankly, that you should be merry—that is, happy and joyous. Not only does it say merrily once, but for greater emphasis (to make sure that you *really* get the point), this word is repeated *four* times.

In exhorting you to be merry as you're rowing gently down the stream, the song implies that your attitude and behavior should be full of fun and laughter, (the dictionary definition) festive, and even celebratory.

The big punch line, of course, comes in the last five words: "Life is but a dream." At the end, it seems, none of it has ever been "real." There never was either a real boat or a real passenger. There wasn't any water and there wasn't any actual journeying down a stream to some final destination. This last line plainly suggests, instead, that *all* of it—boat, passenger, water, and the journey—has only been maya, the Great Illusion.

Amazingly, this same core Truth about the illusory nature of the universe has also been spoken of for centuries by the cross-cultural perennial philosophy.

Isn't it absolutely incredible that such profound wisdom could be successfully distilled into only eighteen simple words, and that it's cleverly disguised now as a simple little ditty that's sung with friends around a campfire?

And isn't it ironic that it took me 757 words to remind you about it?

Chuck Hillig, MFT, is a psychotherapist and the author of several books on eastern philosophy. He has been a devotee of Ramana Maharshi since 1970.

Besides giving lectures and workshops, he is also occasionally available for private consultations in person, over the phone, or even through email. For further information, please contact him at chuck@chuckhillig.com.

Chuck is also the author of:

Enlightenment for Beginners

The Way IT Is

The Magic King

Looking for God

Sentient Publications, LLC publishes books on cultural creativity, experimental education, transformative spirituality, holistic health, new science, ecology, and other topics, approached from an integral viewpoint. Our authors are intensely interested in exploring the nature of life from fresh perspectives, addressing life's great questions, and fostering the full expression of the human potential. Sentient Publications' books arise from the spirit of inquiry and the richness of the inherent dialogue between writer and reader.

Our Culture Tools series is designed to give social catalyzers and cultural entrepreneurs the essential information, technology, and inspiration to forge a sustainable, creative, and compassionate world.

We are very interested in hearing from our readers. To direct suggestions or comments to us, or to be added to our mailing list, please contact:

SENTIENT PUBLICATIONS, LLC

1113 Spruce Street
Boulder, CO 80302
303-443-2188
contact@sentientpublications.com
www.sentientpublications.com

Made in the USA
Monee, IL
13 July 2020

36527400R00154